MILAN KUN_ _____.

The Life and Works of a Literary Maestro

By

Morghan Knight

Table of Contents

Introduction

Milan Kundera, a Czech-French writer, is widely regarded as one of the twentieth century's most influential novelists. Kundera's works have captivated readers all over the world for their masterful blend of philosophy, politics, and psychology. This biography delves into the life and creative journey of a man who pushed literary boundaries, examining his personal experiences, intellectual development, and the profound impact he had on the literary landscape.

Chapter 1

Origins and Early Life

Childhood in Brno, Czechoslovakia

Milan Kundera was born on April 1, 1929, in the vibrant Czechoslovakian city of Brno. Brno, located in the heart of Central Europe, was a city brimming with cultural and intellectual zeal. Kundera's upbringing in this rich environment influenced his artistic sensibilities and lifelong exploration of the human condition.

A fusion of influences marked Kundera's childhood. His father, Ludvik Kundera, was a concert pianist, and his mother, Milada

Kunderova, taught music. Growing up in a musical family, Milan developed a deep appreciation for the arts at a young age. His father's piano harmonies and the melodies that echoed through the family home would later find their way into the intricate symphony of his prose.

Education and Intellectual Awakening

Kundera demonstrated a prodigious intellect as a young student. His academic pursuits led him to Charles University in Prague, where he studied musicology and literature. Kundera's intellectual awakening occurred during his university years, when he immersed himself in the works of great thinkers and philosophers.

In Prague, Kundera met influential mentors and classmates who broadened his horizons. He participated in lively debates on literature, philosophy, and politics, honing his critical thinking skills and honing his literary voice. As he absorbed the literary traditions of Czechoslovakia and beyond, the intellectual climate of Prague in the 1940s and 1950s provided fertile ground for Kundera's burgeoning talents.

During this time, Kundera also experimented with art forms other than literature. He experimented with music composition, adding to the rich tapestry of Prague's artistic community. His exploration of various creative outlets would later manifest itself in the multifaceted nature of his novels, which frequently incorporate elements of music, film, and other artistic disciplines.

Kundera developed a deep appreciation for existentialism through his studies and interactions with other intellectuals, a philosophical movement that would leave an indelible mark on his writing. Among others, the works of Jean-Paul Sartre, Albert Camus, and Martin Heidegger struck a chord with Kundera, sparking a lifelong fascination with the complexities of human existence, freedom, and the search for meaning.

As his intellectual and creative pursuits flourished, Kundera began to develop his distinct literary style, which is distinguished by introspection, irony, and a profound understanding of the human psyche. Little did he realize that his formative years in Brno and Prague were just the beginning of a remarkable literary journey that would captivate readers worldwide and establish him as one of the twentieth century's most influential novelists.

Chapter 2

Artistic Pursuits and the Prague Spring

Exploring Different Art Forms

Milan Kundera's insatiable curiosity and creative spirit led him to experiment with various artistic mediums outside of literature. He experimented with music, film, and collaborative projects as a young artist, which shaped his multidimensional approach to storytelling.

Kundera's musical inclinations, which he inherited from his father, drove him to explore the world of composition. He played with musical structures and motifs, attempting to express emotions and narratives through harmonies and melodies. This musical exploration not only expanded his understanding of artistic expression, but it also influenced his literary style. Kundera's prose has a rhythmic quality to it, evoking a symphony of words that echoes the harmonies he once attempted to create with musical compositions.

Furthermore, Kundera's interest in cinema led him to work in the film industry. He worked on a variety of projects, including screenplays and adaptations, where he honed his visual storytelling skills and gained a better understanding of narrative structure. This venture into film broadened his artistic palette, allowing him to approach his novels with a keen visual sensibility, creating vivid scenes and evocative imagery to bring his narratives to life.

Political Awakening

The 1960s were a watershed moment in Czechoslovakia, both politically and culturally. It was during this period that the Prague Spring, led by Alexander Dubek, emerged as a political reform movement. The Prague Spring was a wave of hope and desire for greater political freedom that challenged the repressive regime of the Soviet-supported Communist Party.

Kundera, like many other artists and intellectuals of his generation, became engulfed in the fervor of this movement. He was a firm believer in the power of art to challenge and question established norms, and he saw the Prague Spring as an opportunity for Czechoslovakia to embrace a more open and democratic society. As he sought to capture the essence of this transformative moment in his works, Kundera's writing became increasingly intertwined with his political beliefs.

The Soviet Invasion and Disillusionment

However, the promising winds of change were abruptly quelled when Soviet forces invaded Czechoslovakia in August 1968, effectively ending the Prague Spring. This repressive act had a profound impact on Kundera and the entire nation. The invasion shattered Kundera's hopes for a more free society, leaving an indelible mark on his psyche and artistic vision.

The experience of the Soviet invasion and its aftermath left Kundera feeling disillusioned. Under the oppressive regime, he witnessed the erosion of personal freedoms and the stifling of artistic expression. This disillusionment seeped into his writing, prompting him to explore themes of political repression, individual liberty, and power dynamics in his novels.

This period's works by Kundera, such as "The Joke" and "Life Is Elsewhere," bear the unmistakable imprint of his disillusionment with totalitarianism. He depicts the struggles of individuals caught in the web of political oppression, their yearning for freedom, and the profound impact that political forces have on their lives through his characters.

The experiences of experimenting with different art forms and witnessing the rise and fall of the Prague Spring, followed by the Soviet invasion, acted as a crucible for Kundera's creative evolution. They influenced his narrative style, imbuing his works with profound depth and an unwavering commitment to exposing the human condition in all its complexities, resilience, and vulnerability.

Chapter 3

Exile and Embracing French Culture

Settling in France

Milan Kundera was disillusioned and disheartened in the aftermath of the Soviet invasion of Czechoslovakia. He made the fateful decision to flee his homeland and seek refuge in France in 1975. This was a watershed moment in Kundera's life and career, as he embarked on a new chapter in a foreign land that would profoundly shape his literary voice.

When Kundera arrived in Paris, he found solace and a sense of belonging in the city's vibrant intellectual and artistic community. The French capital, known for its rich cultural heritage and history of artistic expression, provided a fertile ground for artistic exploration and personal reinvention for Kundera. He would fully embrace French culture and establish himself as a prominent figure in the literary landscape during his time in France.

Assimilation and the French Connection

Assimilation into French society presented difficulties for Kundera. Language barriers and cultural differences were initially obstacles, but his perseverance and love of literature propelled him forward. Kundera immersed himself in French language and culture, diligently honing his linguistic skills and absorbing his adopted country's literary traditions.

Paris served as a testing ground for Kundera's artistic development. He made deep connections with influential French intellectuals, writers, and artists, shaping his worldview and literary sensibilities. Cafés and literary salons provided fertile ground for intellectual discourse, where Kundera exchanged ideas, debated philosophies, and honed his literary voice.

Interactions with French literary luminaries such as Jean-Paul Sartre, Simone de Beauvoir, and Philippe Sollers aided Kundera's assimilation and intellectual development. Their collaborations, discussions, and friendship deepened

Kundera's understanding of existentialism, poststructuralism, and the nuances of French literary theory, all of which found resonance in his own work.

The Impact of French Literature

Kundera's artistic vision was profoundly influenced by French literature. Among others, the works of Marcel Proust, Gustave Flaubert, and Albert Camus captivated him, with their themes of memory, existentialism, and the human condition resonating deeply with his own explorations.

Kundera's prose style and narrative structure show the influence of French literature. He embraced the nuanced and introspective storytelling style, which is distinguished by psychological depth and intricate character studies. His novels, such as "The Unbearable Lightness of Being" and "Immortality," demonstrate a synthesis of French philosophical thought and Central European storytelling traditions, resulting in a distinct blend that transcends national boundaries.

Furthermore, Kundera's immersion in French culture broadened his artistic palette. The vibrant Parisian art scene, with its museums, galleries, and avant-garde movements, served as a constant source of inspiration for him. His writing was influenced by visual arts, music, and cinema, which added layers of complexity and visual imagery to his narratives.

Literary Exile and Identity

Exile and embracing French culture had a profound impact on Kundera's exploration of themes such as identity, displacement, and the search for belonging. As an émigré, he wrestled with issues of cultural heritage and identity fluidity in a globalized world.

In Kundera's novels, characters frequently navigate the complexities of living between cultures, capturing the essence of the immigrant experience and the challenges of reconciling multiple identities. His own experiences as a literary exile have given him keen insights into the human psyche and the ability to depict the nuances of cultural encounters.

Conclusion:

Milan Kundera's decision to leave Czechoslovakia and embrace French culture marked a watershed moment in his life and artistic career. Kundera developed a strong bond with his adopted country through his integration into French society, interactions with French intellectuals, and immersion in the rich tapestry of French literature and arts. His unique literary voice was shaped by the fusion of his Central European roots and French influences, which established him as a global literary figure known for his profound explorations of identity, existentialism, and the complexities of the human condition.

Chapter 4

The Unbearable Lightness of Being

Magnum Opus

"The Unbearable Lightness of Being," published in 1984, is Milan Kundera's magnum opus, a novel that has received critical acclaim as well as a worldwide readership. This seminal work established Kundera as one of the most influential and thought-provoking writers of his generation. This chapter delves into the complexities of this extraordinary novel, examining its philosophical underpinnings, narrative structure, and the long-lasting impact it has had on readers.

Themes and Motifs

"The Unbearable Lightness of Being" is, at its core, a profound exploration of human existence, love, and the search for meaning in a world marked by transience and uncertainty. Kundera interweaves several stories, intertwining the lives of four central characters: Tomas, Tereza, Sabina, and Franz. The novel delves into themes of love, fidelity, freedom, and the inherent paradoxes of human existence through their intertwined stories.

One of the novel's central themes is the concept of "lightness" and "heaviness." Kundera introduces the concept of life being either weightless or burdened with significance. He suggests that lightness represents a carefree existence free of attachments and responsibilities, whereas heaviness is defined by the weight of commitments, choices, and moral implications. Kundera expertly explores the conflict between these opposing forces, inviting readers to consider the consequences of choosing one over the other.

The novel's exploration of individual freedom and its limitations is another recurring theme. Kundera delves into the delicate balance of personal liberty and the interconnectedness of human existence, demonstrating how our decisions and actions affect the lives of others. He questions the concept of absolute freedom, presenting a complex web of interdependencies that shape our decisions and identities.

Narrative Style and Structure

"The Unbearable Lightness of Being" exemplifies Kundera's distinct narrative style, which is distinguished by philosophical musings and profound introspection. He weaves a rich tapestry of thought-provoking ideas into the fictional narrative, historical events, philosophical digressions, and reflective commentary.

The novel is divided into seven sections, each of which explores a different aspect of the characters' lives and the themes at stake. Kundera uses a nonlinear narrative structure, moving back and forth in time with fluidity, blurring the lines between memory, fantasy, and reality. This unconventional approach reflects the complexities of human experience and reinforces the novel's central theme of existence's multifaceted nature.

Kundera's prose is distinguished by its clarity and lyrical beauty. His ability to evoke emotions through vivid descriptions, philosophical insights, and introspective passages transports readers into the inner lives of the characters and invites reflection on the deeper questions that lie at the heart of human existence.

Global Impact and Legacy

"The Unbearable Lightness of Being" struck a chord with readers all over the world, transcending cultural barriers and capturing the essence of the human condition. Its exploration of love, freedom, and the search for meaning struck a chord, especially in a world grappling with modernity's complexities.

The novel's profound impact has lasted over time, firmly establishing its place in the literary canon. It has been translated into numerous languages, earning international acclaim and a devoted following. Kundera's thought-provoking reflections on the nature of existence continue to inspire readers, challenging them to consider the significance and weight of their own lives.

Conclusion:

"The Unbearable Lightness of Being" is a literary masterpiece that exemplifies Milan Kundera's distinct blend of philosophical insight, lyrical prose, and multifaceted storytelling. The novel invites readers to reflect on the complexities of existence and the choices that shape our lives through its exploration of love, freedom, and the human condition. Kundera's magnum opus has left an indelible imprint on literature by providing a profound and timeless exploration of the fundamental questions that define our shared human experience.

Chapter 5

Writing and Reflections

The Art of the Novel

Milan Kundera's literary career is distinguished by a deep dedication to the novel as an art form. This chapter delves into his writing process, narrative techniques, and philosophical underpinnings that lend depth and resonance to his works.

Kundera's approach to the novel is heavily influenced by his musical background and fascination with structure and form. He sees the novel as a word symphony, painstakingly crafting each sentence to achieve a harmonious balance of rhythm, cadence, and meaning. His prose has a musical quality to it, with carefully constructed sentences that flow smoothly, creating a lyrical and immersive reading experience.

Kundera's ability to seamlessly blend different narrative strands, interweaving past and present, reality and imagination, is central to his writing. He uses a fragmented narrative style to reflect the fragmented nature of human memory and perception. This fragmented approach allows Kundera to explore multiple points of view, providing readers with a multifaceted understanding of the complexities of human experience.

Furthermore, Kundera's novels are frequently distinguished by his use of intertextuality. He engages in literary dialogue with other works, quoting and reinterpreting texts from various literary traditions. By incorporating intertextuality into his writing, Kundera connects his own works to the larger literary canon, inviting readers to investigate the interplay of ideas across different literary contexts.

Essays and Literary Criticism

Milan Kundera is well-known for his thought-provoking essays and literary criticism, in addition to his fiction. These nonfiction works provide profound insights into literature, philosophy, and his era's cultural landscape.

Kundera's essays cover a wide range of topics, including the nature of storytelling and the writer's role in society, as well as reflections on memory, history, and the complexities of human relationships. His essays are distinguished by their intellectual rigor, philosophical depth, and ability to elicit debate and introspection.

His literary criticism enlightens the works of other authors by combining analysis, personal reflection, and philosophical inquiry. Kundera's criticisms not only shed light on other writers' creative choices and thematic concerns, but also provide insight into his own artistic sensibilities and the standards by which he evaluates literature.

The Writer's Responsibility

Milan Kundera wrestles with the ethical and moral responsibilities of the writer throughout his writing and reflections. He believes that literature should challenge prevailing norms and ideologies as well as entertain.

Kundera sees the writer as a keeper of memory, tasked with preserving and illuminating humanity's collective experiences. He believes that literature has the power to expose truths, challenge established narratives, and inspire readers to think critically about their own lives and societies.

Kundera believes that the writer must walk a fine line between artistic freedom and ethical obligations. He believes in the importance of challenging authority, opposing oppressive systems, and advocating for individual liberty. However, he recognizes the importance of empathy, compassion, and being aware of the consequences of one's words.

Conclusion

Milan Kundera's approach to writing and reflections exemplifies his deep commitment to the novel as an art form and literature's broader role in society. His meticulous craftsmanship, narrative techniques, and philosophical insights illuminate the human experience, inviting readers to consider profound questions and the complexities of existence. Kundera's writing and reflections are proof of literature's ability to inspire, challenge, and shape our understanding of the world.

Chapter 6

Later Life and Legacy

Kundera's Later Novels

Milan Kundera's later life was defined by his ongoing exploration of the human condition and dedication to his craft. This chapter delves into his post-"Unbearable Lightness of Being" novels, examining themes, stylistic choices, and critical reception.

Following the publication of his magnum opus, Kundera published a number of notable novels, each of which contributed to his illustrious literary legacy. "Immortality" (1990), "Ignorance" (2002), and "The Festival of Insignificance" (2013) are examples of Kundera's ability to delve into profound existential questions while maintaining his signature blend of philosophical insight and lyrical prose.

In *"Immortality,"* Kundera delves into the nature of art, memory, and the search for immortality. The novel intertwines its characters' lives, delving into their personal histories and examining the eternal human desire for lasting significance. Kundera's exploration of memory and its relationship to personal and collective identity strikes a deep chord with readers, prompting them to consider how memory shapes our understanding of ourselves and our place in the world.

"Ignorance" explores themes of nostalgia, exile, and the complexities of returning home. Kundera reflects on his displacement experience and his struggle to reconnect with a place that has undergone profound transformations. He illuminates the profound sense of loss, alienation, and the shifting nature of personal and cultural identity through the introspections and encounters of his characters.

In "The Festival of Insignificance," Kundera explores the modern world and the triviality of existence in a reflective and satirical manner. The novel examines the everyday routines and obsessions that shape our lives, questioning the significance we ascribe to the mundane, with a blend of humor and philosophical depth.

Awards and Accolades

Milan Kundera's literary contributions have been widely recognized and celebrated. He has received numerous awards and accolades throughout his career, confirming his lasting impact on the literary landscape.

Kundera received the Jerusalem Prize in 1981, which honors writers whose work addresses themes of human freedom, society, and the relationship between individuals and their surroundings. This prestigious award recognized Kundera's ability to capture the complexities of human existence as well as his dedication to investigating the profound questions that shape our lives.

Furthermore, Kundera's influence peaked in 2019 when he was awarded the Nobel Prize in Literature. The Nobel committee praised his "novels of the human being in the widest sense," praising his ability to combine philosophical depth and poetic sensibility in his explorations of the modern condition.

Literary Influence and Legacy

Milan Kundera's literary influence extends well beyond his own works. His perceptive examinations of the human psyche, existential themes, and relationship complexities have left an indelible mark on contemporary literature.

Kundera's ability to blend philosophy, psychology, and storytelling has influenced a new generation of writers seeking to understand the complexities of the human condition. His distinct narrative style, which is distinguished by introspection, intertextuality, and a lyrical quality, continues to captivate readers and aspiring writers alike.

Kundera's works have also been widely translated and have a global readership. His exploration of universal themes and examination of the human experience transcend cultural and geographical boundaries, making him appcaling to readers from all walks of life.

Conclusion

Milan Kundera's later life and legacy bear witness to his unwavering dedication to the craft of writing as well as his exploration of profound existential questions. He continued to push the boundaries of literary storytelling in his later novels, inviting readers to reflect on memory, identity, and the transient nature of human existence. His honors and awards, including the Nobel Prize in Literature, attest to his long-lasting influence on the literary world. Kundera's legacy is found not only in his own works, but also in the inspiration he has provided to subsequent generations of writers, who continue to be inspired by his profound insights and distinct narrative style.

Health & Death

It is unclear what exactly caused Milan Kundera's death. He had reportedly been battling a long-term illness. The Milan

Kundera Library in Brno, where he was born and raised, acknowledged his death but provided no further details.

As a result, neither the nature of his illness nor the circumstances surrounding his death are known. Such information is frequently kept private in order to respect the privacy of the deceased and their family. The focus remains on Kundera's outstanding literary achievements and his long-standing reputation as a well-known and significant author.

Summary

"Milan Kundera: The Life and Works of a Literary Maestro" is a comprehensive biography that delves into the captivating life and creative journey of Milan Kundera, a Czech-French writer who stands as one of the most influential novelists of the 20th century.

The book traces Kundera's origins and early life in Brno, Czechoslovakia, exploring his formative years and the cultural atmosphere that shaped his artistic sensibilities. It delves into his education, intellectual awakening, and the mentors who influenced his literary development. From his studies in musicology to his encounters with influential intellectuals, readers gain insights into the foundations of Kundera's unique writing style.

As the biography progresses, it delves into Kundera's artistic pursuits and his involvement in the Prague Spring, a movement for political reform in Czechoslovakia. It explores his exploration of different art forms, such as music and film, and how these experiences influenced his multidimensional approach to storytelling. The book also examines the impact of the Prague Spring and subsequent Soviet invasion on Kundera's worldview and writing, unraveling the disillusionment that marked this period of his life.

A significant portion of the biography is dedicated to Kundera's exile and his embrace of French culture. It highlights his settling in France, his assimilation into French society, and his engagement with influential French intellectuals. Readers gain a deep understanding of the fusion between Kundera's Central European roots and the French influences that shaped his literary voice. The exploration of his immersion in French literature and arts reveals how these cultural experiences enriched his artistic palette.

The biography pays special attention to Kundera's magnum opus, "The Unbearable Lightness of Being." It examines the philosophical underpinnings and narrative structure of this renowned novel, exploring its themes of love, freedom, and the search for meaning. The book also discusses Kundera's later works, including "Immortality," "Ignorance," and "The Festival of Insignificance," and their contributions to his literary legacy.

Moreover, the biography sheds light on Kundera's writing process, narrative techniques, and the philosophical insights that infuse his works. It explores his essays and literary criticism, providing a deeper understanding of his reflections on literature, art, and the role of the writer in society.

The later chapters of the book focus on Kundera's later life, the recognition he received through awards such as the Jerusalem Prize and the Nobel Prize in

Literature, and his lasting legacy. It highlights his profound influence on contemporary literature, the global reach of his works, and the inspiration he continues to provide to aspiring writers.

In summary, "Unveiling Milan Kundera: The Life and Works of a Literary Maestro" is a comprehensive biography that offers readers an intimate and detailed exploration of Milan Kundera's life, creative journey, and lasting impact on the literary world. It takes readers on a remarkable voyage through the personal experiences, intellectual development, and profound insights of a writer whose works continue to captivate and inspire readers worldwide.

Printed in Great Britain
by Amazon

39650699R00030